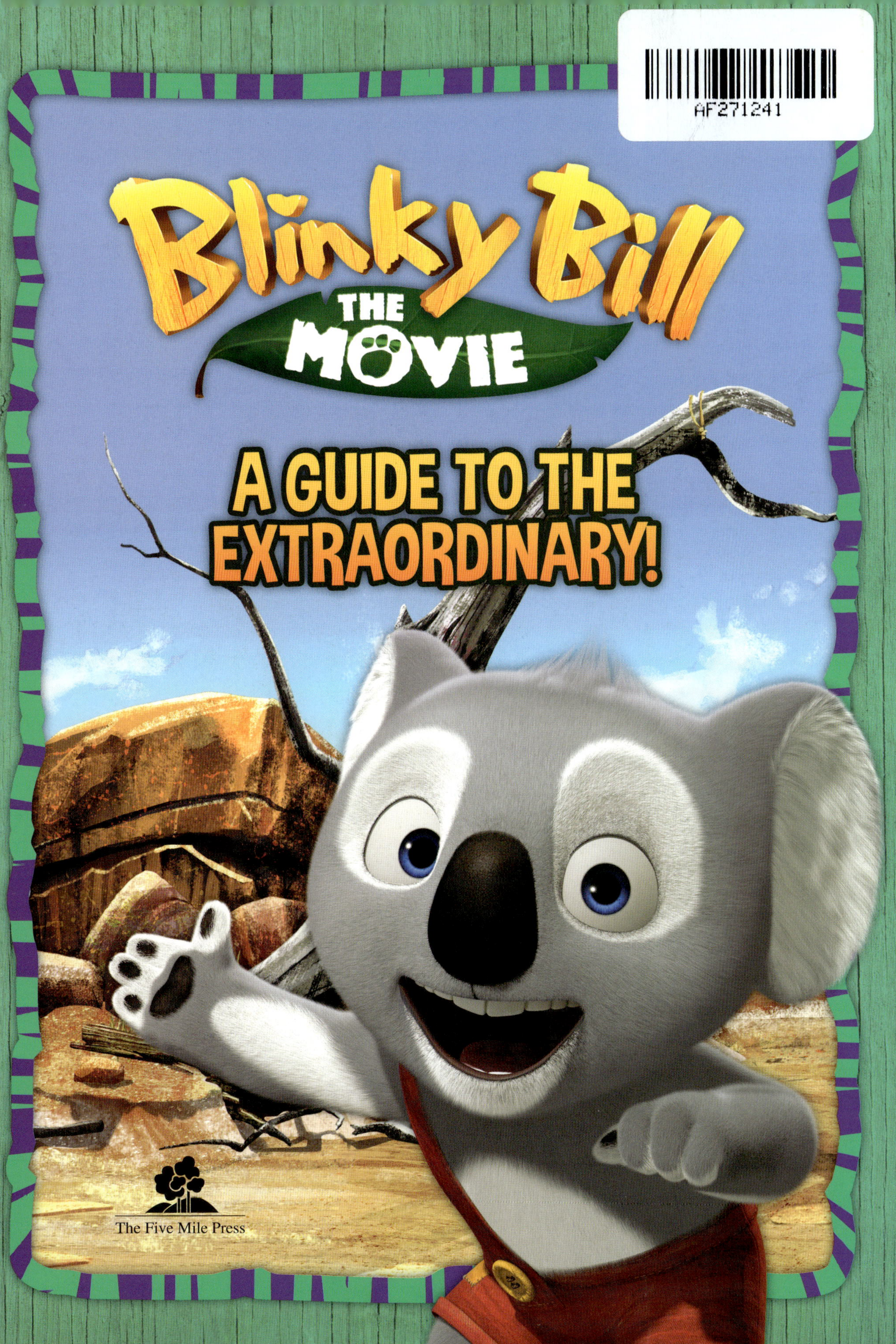
Blinky Bill
THE MOVIE
A GUIDE TO THE EXTRAORDINARY!
The Five Mile Press

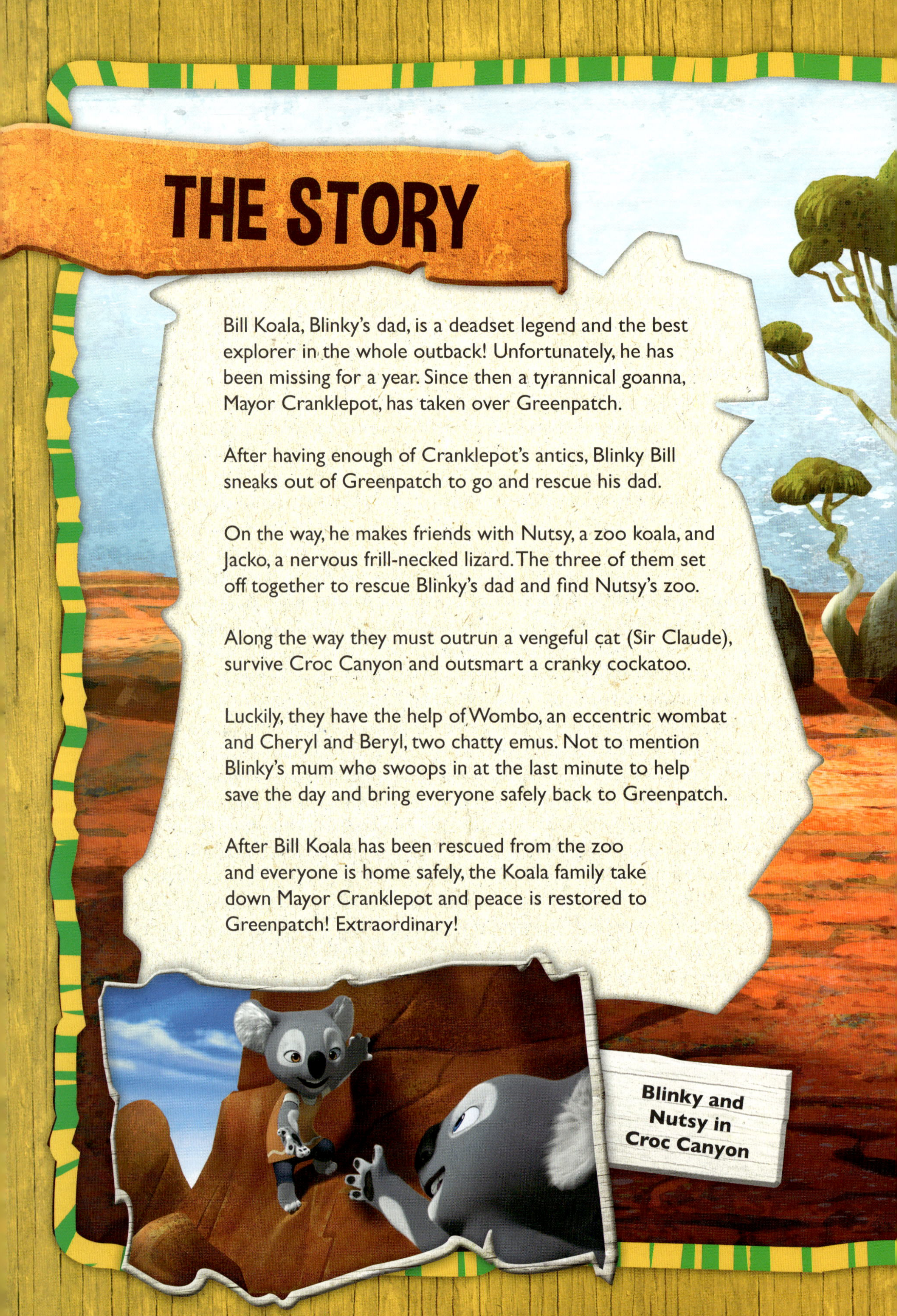

THE STORY

Bill Koala, Blinky's dad, is a deadset legend and the best explorer in the whole outback! Unfortunately, he has been missing for a year. Since then a tyrannical goanna, Mayor Cranklepot, has taken over Greenpatch.

After having enough of Cranklepot's antics, Blinky Bill sneaks out of Greenpatch to go and rescue his dad.

On the way, he makes friends with Nutsy, a zoo koala, and Jacko, a nervous frill-necked lizard. The three of them set off together to rescue Blinky's dad and find Nutsy's zoo.

Along the way they must outrun a vengeful cat (Sir Claude), survive Croc Canyon and outsmart a cranky cockatoo.

Luckily, they have the help of Wombo, an eccentric wombat and Cheryl and Beryl, two chatty emus. Not to mention Blinky's mum who swoops in at the last minute to help save the day and bring everyone safely back to Greenpatch.

After Bill Koala has been rescued from the zoo and everyone is home safely, the Koala family take down Mayor Cranklepot and peace is restored to Greenpatch! Extraordinary!

BLINKY BILL

Blinky Bill is a koala on a mission! Nothing will stop this adventurer from finding his dad.

Blinky lives with his mum, Dorothy Koala, in Greenpatch Village. But things haven't been going smoothly since Blinky's dad went missing a year ago. Blinky wants to find his dad and thinks his mum has given up. So he sneaks out of Greenpatch and sets off on the adventure of a lifetime!

BLINKY'S STATS

Mission: To find Bill Koala, aka Dad
Personality: Cheeky and kind-hearted
Arch enemies: Mayor Cranklepot & Sir Claude
Special talent: Escaping danger!

Blinky's home

Blinky tries to convince Nutsy he is an accomplished tracker.

NUTSY

This quick-witted, fast-talking koala is thrust into Blinky's adventure when he 'rescues' her from the back of a ute. Nutsy is on her way to a new zoo – and she is not happy about being lost in the bush with a wild koala who, on first impressions, is a bumbling bumpkin!

Despite her zoo upbringing, Nutsy is brave, strong and smart!

NUTSY'S STATS

Mission: To find her zoo
Personality: Street smart
Biggest threat: Sir Claude
Special talent: Embracing adventure!

Blinky 'rescuing' Nutsy
That sweaty
unwashed smell ...
you're wild!
Getting to know each other
Nutsy getting
acquainted
with bush life.

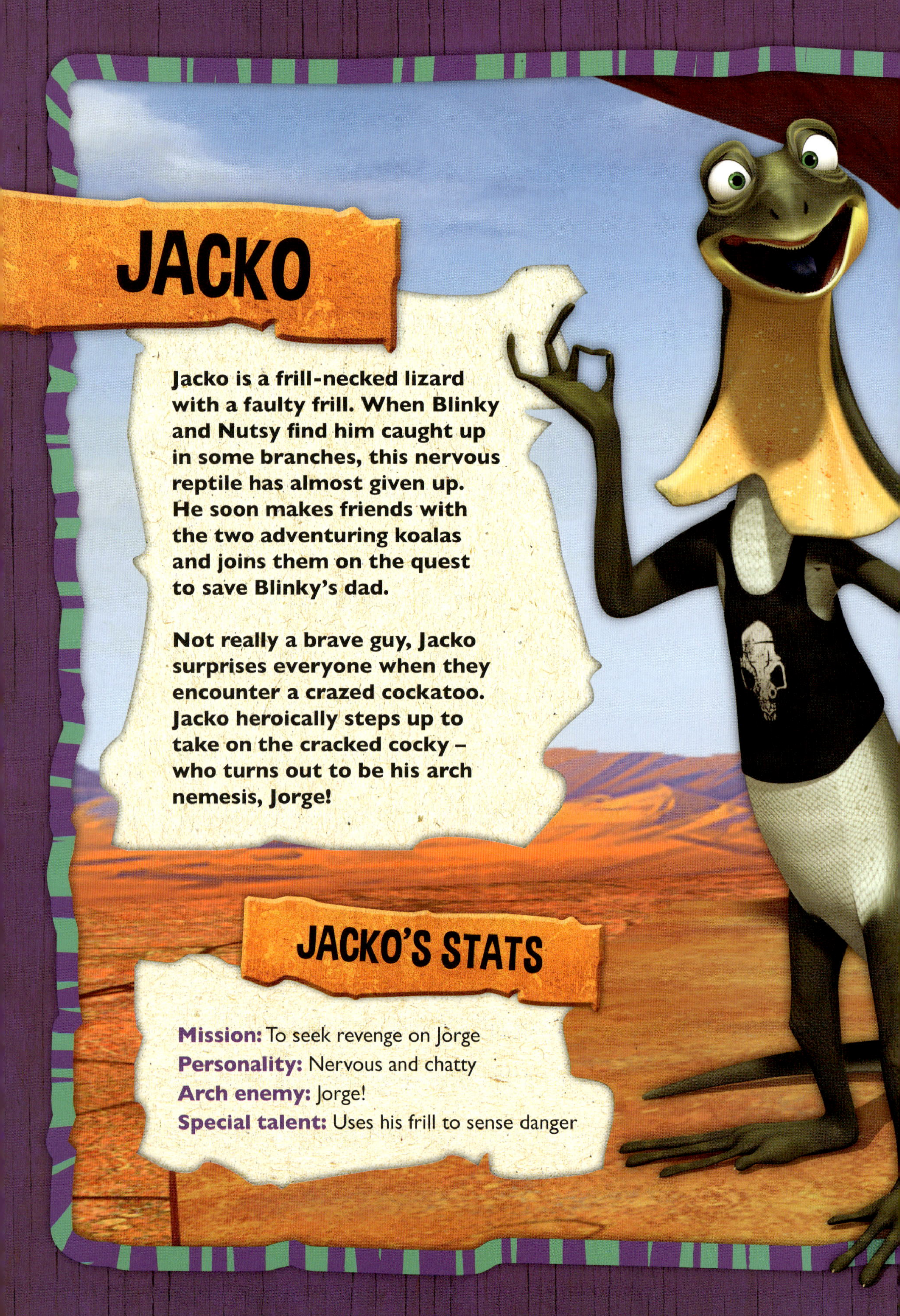

JACKO

Jacko is a frill-necked lizard with a faulty frill. When Blinky and Nutsy find him caught up in some branches, this nervous reptile has almost given up. He soon makes friends with the two adventuring koalas and joins them on the quest to save Blinky's dad.

Not really a brave guy, Jacko surprises everyone when they encounter a crazed cockatoo. Jacko heroically steps up to take on the cracked cocky – who turns out to be his arch nemesis, Jorge!

JACKO'S STATS

Mission: To seek revenge on Jorge
Personality: Nervous and chatty
Arch enemy: Jorge!
Special talent: Uses his frill to sense danger

Jacko claims to be the greatest tracker in the bush.

Blinky's best friends and partners in crime are Robert, Marcia and Splodge. These three Greenpatchians look up to Blinky as their leader and are key players in his schemes to bring down Mayor Cranklepot.

Robert, Marcia and Splodge are caught in the act by Blinky's mum!

'A hundred yams says he's back before lunch.'

This mouse likes to over-dramatise for her own amusement. She loves her friends but doesn't mind taking a bet against them if she spots good odds.

MARCIA

'What? Kangaroos hop, lyrebirds mimic! Deal with it.'

Robert is a lyrebird and master impersonator. He can mimic any sound: monsters, sirens, falling paddy melons – you name it, he can mimic it.

ROBERT

'But, Blinky, what if …?'

This kangaroo doesn't have a mean bone in his body and is the kind of guy you want as a friend. He can be wary of Blinky's schemes but is always supportive in the end.

SPLODGE

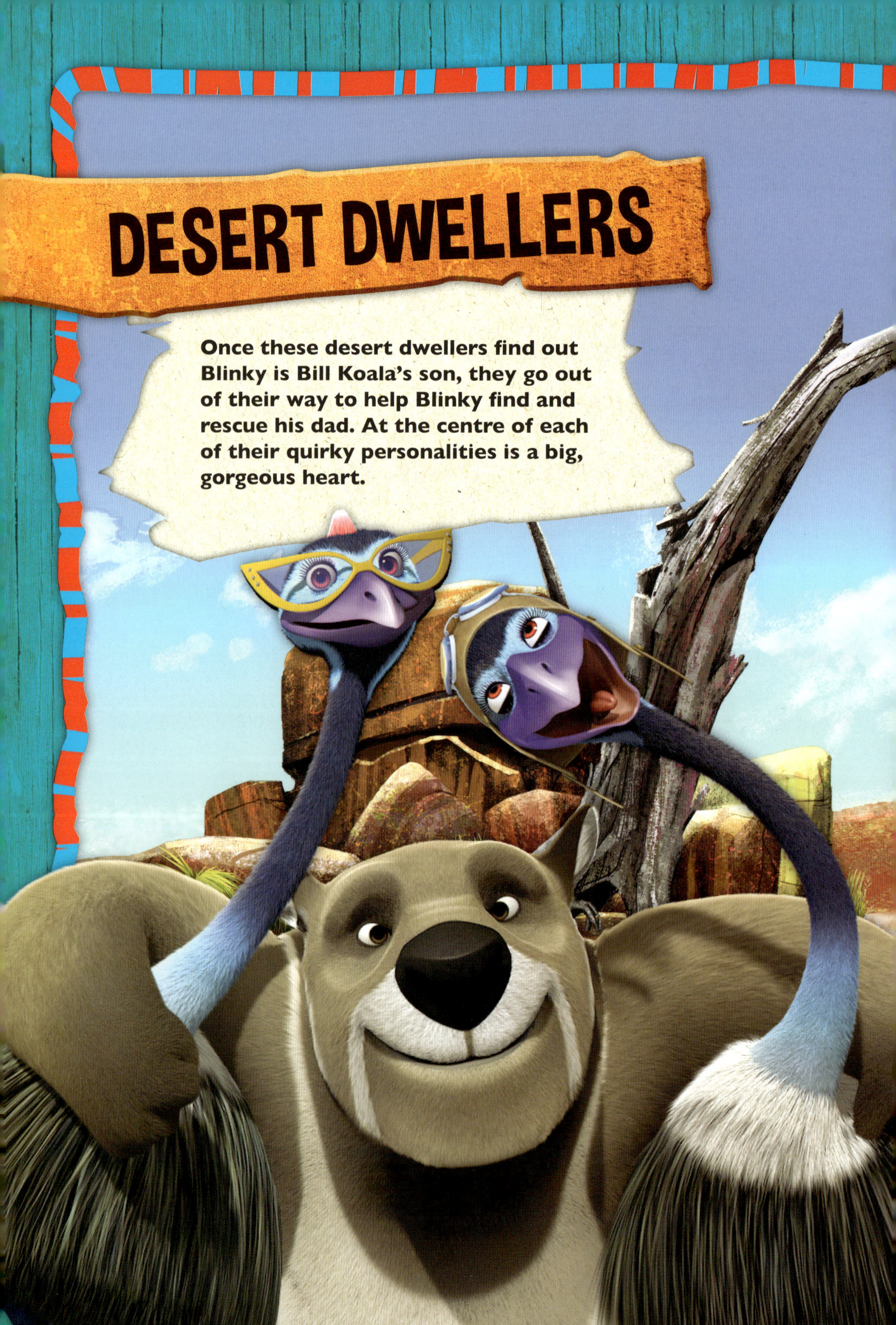

DESERT DWELLERS

Once these desert dwellers find out Blinky is Bill Koala's son, they go out of their way to help Blinky find and rescue his dad. At the centre of each of their quirky personalities is a big, gorgeous heart.

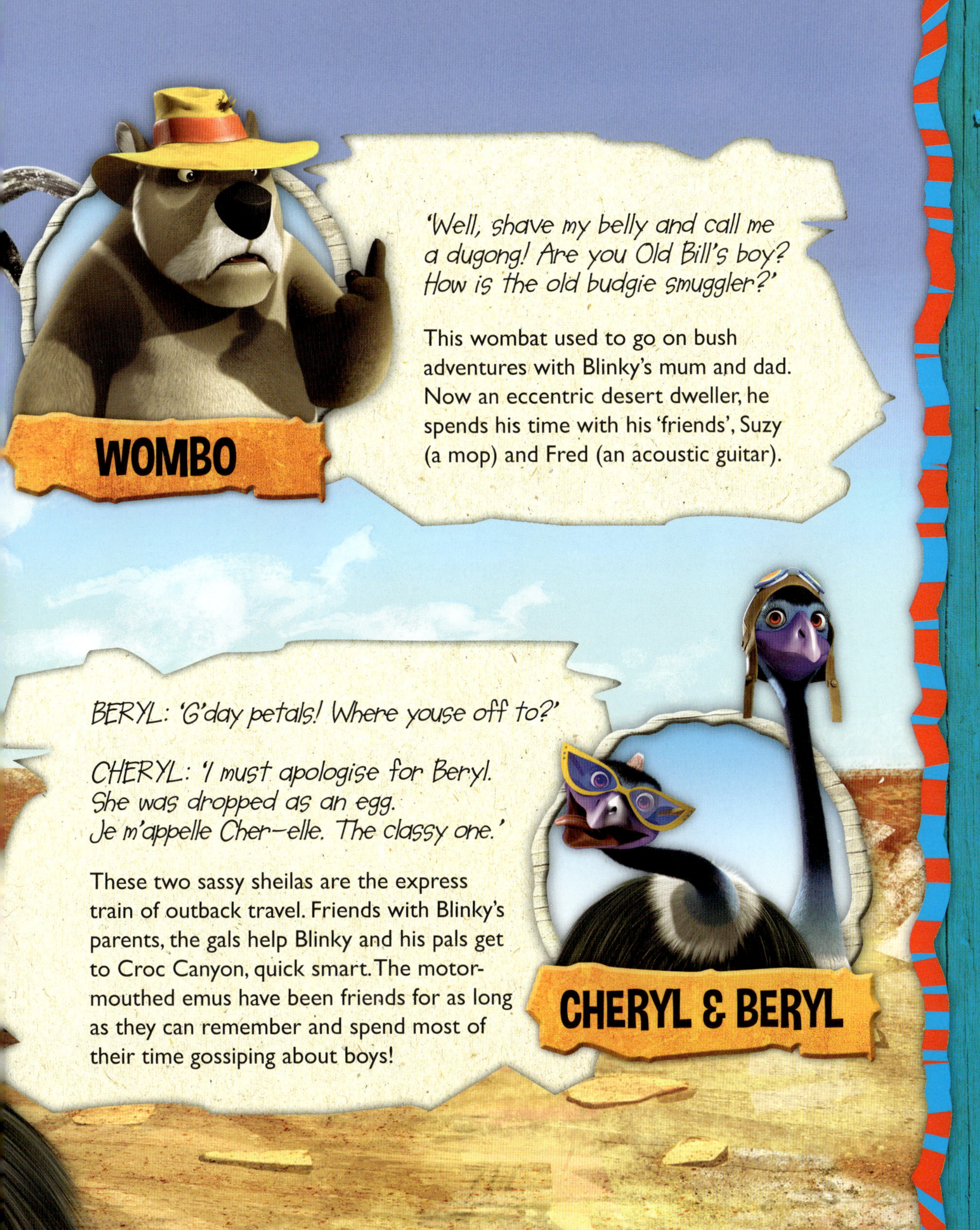

'Well, shave my belly and call me a dugong! Are you Old Bill's boy? How is the old budgie smuggler?'

This wombat used to go on bush adventures with Blinky's mum and dad. Now an eccentric desert dweller, he spends his time with his 'friends', Suzy (a mop) and Fred (an acoustic guitar).

WOMBO

BERYL: 'G'day petals! Where youse off to?'

CHERYL: 'I must apologise for Beryl. She was dropped as an egg. Je m'appelle Cher–elle. The classy one.'

These two sassy sheilas are the express train of outback travel. Friends with Blinky's parents, the gals help Blinky and his pals get to Croc Canyon, quick smart. The motor-mouthed emus have been friends for as long as they can remember and spend most of their time gossiping about boys!

CHERYL & BERYL

BILL & DOROTHY KOALA

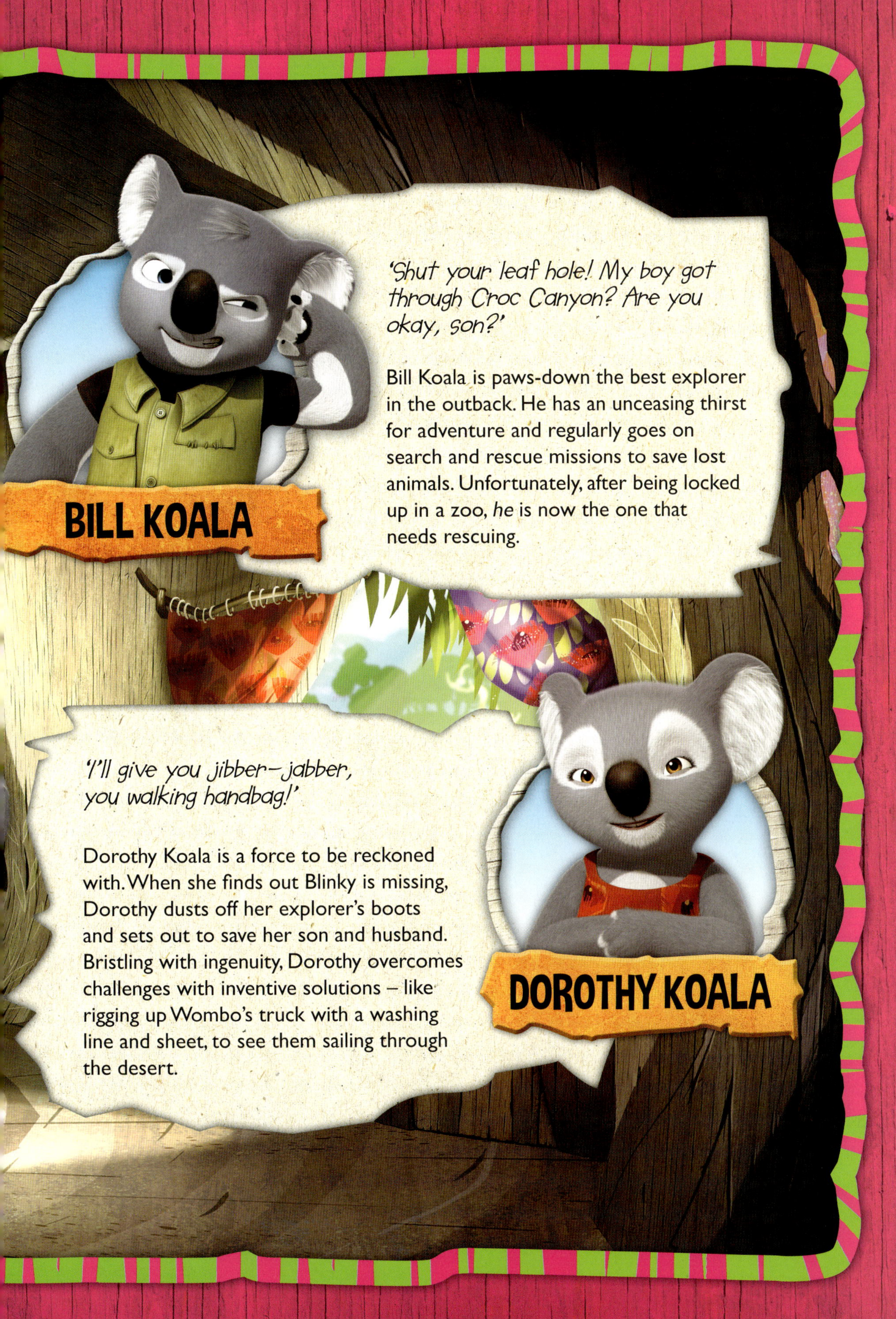

BILL KOALA

'Shut your leaf hole! My boy got through Croc Canyon? Are you okay, son?'

Bill Koala is paws-down the best explorer in the outback. He has an unceasing thirst for adventure and regularly goes on search and rescue missions to save lost animals. Unfortunately, after being locked up in a zoo, *he* is now the one that needs rescuing.

DOROTHY KOALA

'I'll give you jibber-jabber, you walking handbag!'

Dorothy Koala is a force to be reckoned with. When she finds out Blinky is missing, Dorothy dusts off her explorer's boots and sets out to save her son and husband. Bristling with ingenuity, Dorothy overcomes challenges with inventive solutions — like rigging up Wombo's truck with a washing line and sheet, to see them sailing through the desert.

THE BADDIES

These baddies range from mildly erratic to down right evil. From threatening the peaceful existence of Greenpatch Village to embarking on a vengeful quest to kill off innocent koalas, these meanies are all types of bad.

SCALE OF BADNESS

Selfish and arrogant

Pure Evil

'No escape. If I don't get out ... nobody does!'

This patchily-feathered bird is an ex-friend of Jacko. Once, they were as close as brothers, but after a misunderstanding over a lady, this cocky went crackers.

JORGE

'It's a disgrace! As your king I demand punishment forthwith!'

Mayor Cranklepot is the self-appointed mayor of Greenpatch. This maniacal goanna has gotten too big for his boots and thinks his ludicrous rules will save Greenpatch.

MAYOR CRANKLEPOT

'Time for you to die!'

Sir Claude is one foul-tempered feline who considers himself above native animals. A sticky run in with Blinky's dad has left this cat with a nasty attitude towards koalas – he wants to kill them all!

SIR CLAUDE

HUMAN ENCOUNTERS

Humans are strange creatures that leave their rubbish to clog up bushland and waterways. They try to help animals by locking them in zoos and drive strange machines that can squash animals flat.

Blinky trying out human food. Little does he know these gumnut-shaped goodies are HOT!

Blinky's first sighting of human civilisation.
KOALA JOE'S ROADHOUSE
DINE-IN
KOALA JOE'S
TASTY
NEXT 42 km
NEXT 42 km
This human-made gully is where Blinky first meets Sir Claude!
A small selection of weird human food.
Everybody's favourite breakfast.
MRS PIMMS
MRS PIMMS
snacks
POPCORN
MRS PIMMS
canned food
baked beans
MRS PIMMS
olive oil
MRS PIMMS
lime soda
TUNA

BUSH CRICKET

THE COMMENTATORS

Seasoned commentators, Richie and Tony, keep the crowds up to date on the latest cricket action.

THE PLAYERS

While bush cricket is open to all, crickets themselves are the main players.

THE HAZARDS OF THE GAME

When the players are crickets and the commentators are kookaburras, well … let's listen in to see what could happen …

Richie: *And what a thrilling test it's been, Tony! Eight hours of play and not a single run scored! You could cut the tension with your beak!*

Tony: *If it was any more absorbing it would be a tea towel! And … my, aren't the players looking delicious this afternoon.*

Richie: *They certainly are, Tony! I'd lick my lips if I had any …*